*Philosopher Kings*

There will be no end to the troubles of states, or of humanity itself, till philosophers become kings in this world, or till those we now call kings and rulers really and truly become philosophers, and political power and philosophy thus come into the same hands.  ~ ***Plato***

*Philosopher Kings*

# Philosopher Kings

## Cara Losier Chanoine

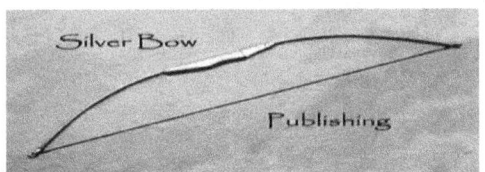

Box 5 – 720 – 6th Street,
New Westminster, BC
V3C 3C5   CANADA

Title: Philosopher Kings
Author: Cara Losier Chanoine
Cover Painting: "Ballerina Dreams" by Candice James
Layout/Design: Candice James
Editing: Candice James

All rights reserved including the right to reproduce or translate this book or any portions thereof, in any form except for the use of short passages for review purposes, no part of this book may be reproduced, in part or in whole, or transmitted in any form or by any means, electronically or mechanically, including photocopying, recording, or any information or storage retrieval system without prior permission in writing from the publisher or a license from the Canadian Copyright Collective Agency (Access Copyright).

ISBN: 9781774032510 Print
ISBN: 9781774032527 eBook
© 2023 Silver Bow Publishing

Library and Archives Canada Cataloguing in Publication

Title: Philosopher kings / Cara Losier Chanoine.
Names: Chanoine, Cara Losier, author.
Description: Poems.
Identifiers: Canadiana (print) 2023013985X | Canadiana (ebook) 20230139906 | ISBN 9781774032510
   (softcover) | ISBN 9781774032527 (Kindle)
Classification: LCC PS3603.H36 P55 2023 | DDC 811/.6—dc23

*To anyone who has taught me anything at all,
with gratitude*

*Philosopher Kings*

# CONTENTS

Toward Sentience / 9
Knockers / 10
Ground Control. / 11
Lunkers / 13
Oscillating Frequencies /14
Welcome to Civilization / 16
The Poet at Eighteen / 17
Allotment / 19
kindred is a word for god / 20
Tintinnabulation / 21
Feast / 22
Drugstore Banquet / 23
Break, Definition Of / 24
Green Monday / 26
A Terrible Beauty / 28
Threnody / 29
Breakfast of Lunatics / 30
Alternate Ending / 32
Blue Notes / 33
Beyond the Cut Mark / 34
Beauty Marks / 35
Tracey: An Elegy / 36
Relearning the Body After Rape / 37
Radiotoxin / 39
Grasshopper Mouse / 40
Lamb's Blood / 41
A Spell for Victor Frankenstein / 43
Allegiance / 45
Alpha Centauri / 46
Armadillo Heart / 47
Documents of Barbarism / 48
Sums and Parts / 50
Imaginary Numbers / 52
Flight Plan / 54
Hometown / 55
Emblems of Grief / 56
Today's Brass Tacks / 57
Pocket Watch / 58

In Context / 59
Lawn Ornaments / 60
Scrapper / 61
Fever Dreams / 62
Friday Service at the Caffeine Cathedral / 63
Small-Town Murder Cowboy / 64
The Patron Saints of Coffee Cups / 65
Our Lady of Libations / 66
The Garden at Dawn / 67
Praying at the Altar of Fruition / 68
One More Rough Beast / 69
Fool's Mate / 70
Elegy for Dead Architecture / 71
To Call the Muse / 73
The Girl Who Spoke Albatross / 75
Nor'easter / 76
Fighting Words / 77
Lazarus Season / 78
Tires for Tombstones / 79
Coppers / 80
Flux / 81
Cartography / 82
Amorphous Relics / 84
Elegy for Boots / 85

Acknowledgments / 86

Author Profile / 87

## **Toward Sentience**

At the campus gallery,
faces rise,
with closed eyes
and open mouths,
from a tapestry of boiled wool.


They boast full cheeks
and fine foreheads,
teased into dimension
by a careful hand.


They rise,
like anything imprisoned,
toward the possibility of existence.

## Knockers

We used to play thirty-one
        for pennies
around the dining room table,
except we always called it Scat.

My mother passed out custard cups
        to hold the pennies,
and the grown-ups drank
cheap red wine and talked
at an ever-escalating volume
        while the overhead light
          yellowed the room
  against the encroaching nightfall.

I liked the game because its rules
        were simple enough
          for my child's mind
            to grasp
  and my fingers could manage
        the three-card hands.

At the end of the night,
I would feed my winnings
to a plastic pony bank.

The weight of twenty
  or thirty pennies
in my small hand always felt
so much more substantial
than it had any reason to.

## Ground Control

I wanted to be an astronaut
      at five;
rocket launch footage
scrolled behind my closed eyelids
as I slipped into sleep.

We made growth charts at school,
and mine had a paper space helmet
      at the top,
like a finish line trophy.


One day, my grandmother told me
about the Challenger disaster.
How the shuttle burst into flames
      like a funeral pyre
and a New Hampshire girl
        (like me)
was seared into the sky.

I imagined what it was like
to die so far above everything
signifies humanity.


I fell asleep with explosions behind my eyelids.
I dreamed of an infinite, soundless vacuum
      and woke up breathless.
It was the first time my fear was practical.
      It was the first hatchet mark
      in the tree of my childhood.


    I did not become
      an astronaut.
That first adult experience of fear
cut that branch of my childhood
      clean off.

*Philosopher Kings*

I have taken other risks,
am brave in other ways,
but sometimes I dream of shuttle takeoffs,
and I wonder about foolish things
like destiny and accident.

The grainy footage projects
across my brain,
and I mouth the numbers
counting

        d
           o
              w
                 n

                     to liftoff.

## **Lunkers**

When I was young,
I used to throw back
all my uncle's newly caught fish
when he took me along on fishing trips.

One time,
he strung his catches onto a slender branch,
threading it through all the pairs of gills.

I worked one loose
and tried to set it free.

I held it in the shallows of the river
        and let the
          *c u r r e n t*
        filter water
       through its gills,
   but it was already too late.

## Oscillating Frequencies

The theremin
looks less like a musical instrument
than it does a transistor radio,
or a telegraph machine,
or the black boxes that survive plane crashes.


      It has antennae,
like it could pick up lost broadcasts,
like it might be something extraterrestrial.
      One controls pitch,
        and one controls volume.

To play the theremin,
you do not touch it.

Instead, you must choreograph the movement
of your hands around the antennae
in nuanced measures.

To play the theremin,
you must make music of thin air,
never sure if you are transmitter
      or receiver.


      Sometimes,
      I think I've been trying
      to play the theremin
      my whole life.


When I was ten,
I began to play the flute.
I learned to kiss the metal lips
      of its mouthpiece,
I learned the black and white charts
that my fingers translated into changing notes.

I made its keys fit my fingertips.
It was music I could feel
       in my mouth,
       in my hands.
It demanded no acts of faith.


When I reach for a note,
while playing the theremin,
I cannot see the precise place
where my hands need to go.

I cannot touch with the skin
of my fingers.

       The intangibility
   is the most frustrating,
         terrifying,
       exhilarating
thing about this act of music.

There is something in me
that knows how different shades
       of movement
will translate into sound.


It is an act of faith
to trust yourself beyond
what you can see
              or feel
                      or hear.

## Welcome to Civilization

At night, it's quiet enough
to hear the humming of the power lines.
It's why she lives on this mountain.
This is what she tells me,
while we sit outside in the viscous dark.


She says nothing of the buried child,
tucked beneath the sod
in a cemetery three states away.


Behind us, her house rises
like something that has always been here,
tucked into the grade and weathered
like the trunks of the surrounding trees.

Inside, the pale, unfinished woodwork looks raw,
like the sap might still be fresh in its grain.
The floorboards have been sanded by the grit
of other people's boots,
relics of nights spent elbow-to-elbow
around the kitchen table,
drinking whiskey and trying to remember
old card games.


Later, I stretch out on a thin mattress
in a twin bed frame,
draped in a clean but threadbare quilt.

The power lines sing like sirens,
like the keening of a bereft mother
who has borne her grief to a higher altitude,
who finds something bearable
in the rarified air.

## The Poet at Eighteen

wrote everything by hand
in a notebook bound in black velvet
and gilded her words in earnest
and unbearable melodrama


gave birth to language
in erratic moments of uncontrolled fever
like something rabid
in the throes of a painful contortion


wore a black trench coat
a size too large
and sat in the windowsill
of her dorm room
listening to Spineshank
and trying not to be so insecure
and wishing not to be so insecure


stood outside with her friends
while they smoked clove cigarettes


cultivated a taste for insomnia


had a boyfriend
who was much bigger
and much angrier
than she was


was always a little surprised
anyone liked her at all

sat in poetry workshops, nauseous
in anticipation of being exposed as a fraud
discomposed by how much smarter and better
everyone else seemed,
and trying not to be so insecure,
and wishing not to be so insecure


the poet at eighteen
took everything too seriously
and walked headlong into clichés
and ate too much candy
and read through the night instead of sleeping
and fell asleep in the library's green easy chairs
          ... and kept writing

## **Allotment**

       I slept exclusively
          in twin beds
for the first twenty-one years of my life:
first, in a small bedroom in my parents' house
and then in a series of equally small dorm rooms.

My childhood room wouldn't accommodate
       a larger bed,
and I never really grew large enough
       to need one.


After college,
I bought a double bed for the first
in a long string of bad apartments.
When I slept in its middle,
I couldn't reach the edges
with my fingers or toes.


        I never knew
   I could spread so far.

          never knew
   I belonged on such a broad canvas.


It took years to adjust to the idea
 I could take up more space
      than I needed.

## kindred is a word for god

Meaghan came to visit me
when I first moved away.

We walked two miles downtown
and found a bar that didn't check IDs.

On the way home,
my sandal strap broke
while we were crossing the bridge,
and I flung the useless shoe into the river.

Meaghan took her shoes off
and walked barefoot with me
through the worst parts of the city.

      We slept in my bed
with our dirty feet tangled in the sheets.

## Tintinnabulation

The violent aversion
to certain shades of sound
is called misophonia.


It is passing sirens,
the waterspray walls
from car tires through puddles,
the clatter of dishes in a waterless sink.
It is the metallic clangor of the garbage truck
upending the parking lot dumpster.


It feels like
atomic disarticulation,
like looking at the inside-out face
of a china doll
through the back of its shattered head.


It feels like
the strange nausea of the moments
between seeing and comprehending
the truly grotesque.


It is an exposed wire in the brain,
unprotected and unpredictable.
There is no repairing it;
there is just the rubber strap
     of endurance
     to bite down upon
while the shock passes through.

## Feast

On the night of my grandmother's funeral,
I sat with my family
in the kitchen of the apartment
she had lived in since I was young.

The drop-leaf table was covered
by an array of casseroles,
each in its own Pyrex casket.
Foil-capped plasticware
lined the chipped Formica countertops.

These were the eulogies
the church could not contain,
the prayers that transcended religion.

After we held the wake,
and placed the pall,
and lowered the casket
into the cold ground,
we crowded into my grandmother's kitchen
like shipwreck survivors
stumbling into the shallows
at the lip of a kind island.

We sought to sate
our hollow hunger
because it was a place to start.


It was an act of resilience,
of remembrance.


It was a kind of ceremony.

## Drugstore Banquet

When I was eighteen,
and my roommate wanted to kill herself,
she left a note where she knew I would find it.

It was covered in a mosaic of pills,
far ranging in opacity and hue.
When I returned to the room with help,
the note was gone.
The pills had been dumped into a plastic bowl
printed with cartoon characters.

Not all cries for help are in languages I understand.

Later, when she was expelled from school,
I felt the requisite regret for being unable
to translate her disturbances
in a way that might have mattered.

When I think of her now,
        in passing,
    I wonder if she's alive,
and whether she still stacks pills in cereal bowls,
      like breakfast rations
   for the last day she'll ever have.


     Like last resorts
in case she lasts too long.

## Break, Definition Of

1. verb-
to rupture sharply, detach crudely
    from the whole;
    to separate into pieces
    that can or cannot be rearticulated
*Example:*
When I received the news,
    filtered through the telephone receiver,
    I dropped a full glass of water,
    cringed in anticipation,
    but somehow, it didn't
    break.

2. verb-
    to violate
    the integrity of;
    to invalidate, through transgression,
    something once impermeable;
    to destroy the boundaries
    that keep one thing from bleeding into all others
*Example:*
    It was a collection of moments
    that made my illusion of safety
    break:
    when the headlights spilled like theater spots
        onto the sidewalk,
    when my leg was pinned beneath a tire,
    when I opened my eyes again,
    when he did not open his.

3. noun-
    a discontinuation of the usual;
    a suspension of effort;
    a reprieve
*Example:*
    Since the moment of the unshattered water glass,
    there has been no break in the ferocity of my grief.

4. verb-
> to ameliorate the intensity of;
> to hinder
> in speed or force;
> to fight against,
> like stream-swimming salmon

*Example:*
> There is no forest of platitudes
> dense enough to break the impact
> of a single person's absence.

5. verb-
> to render ineffective; to disarm;
> to dispatch with claw, and tooth, and venom

*Example:*
> One cannot veto the necessity of mourning,
> of being disemboweled
> by the moving hands on a clock.
> This is how we atone for allowing ourselves to forget
> the mutability of our species,
> but like everything that belongs to us,
> this, too, is transient.
> Our mercy will rise against our penance,
> will break it,
> so what's left of us can survive.

## Green Monday

there is a bomb
that blooms green in the street
rips up the asphalt and settles,
like the green pallor
of death-rattle sickness
like a green day in April
built from runners' tangled legs
and Jackson Pollack vomit stains
green like spoiled, severed limbs
like the tarnished fixtures
of tea chests in the harbor


this is the shrapnel
the skin heals over
green like when you open your eyes
at the bottom of a pool—
and it burns like that, too
whenever someone puts their thumbs
in your scars
pinches the pale of your bruises
as a reminder
like you could possibly forget
like that busted-open street
isn't branded onto the insides of your eyelids
green paint on red canvas,
red blood tipping green leaves
in April


this is how some people learn
what to hate
and it must be simpler for them
but there is no logic in chaos
no formula for safety
and sometimes maybe we'd like a world
with more certainty
but we cannot separate it

back into primary colors
this precarious green thing
balanced upon the precipice
of two extremes


now
a green dusk sets
upon the street
and the ghosts of amputees
lurk in the long, green shadows
but people walk here
like they can't see the scars

## A Terrible Beauty

There is a place
where the Pemigewasset River
drools onto an inlet of rock and sand,
before waking to find it has become
a frenzy of rapids.

It is the border of a constant tempest,
a place of precarious and transitory peace.
Some people call it beautiful.

They come with beach towels
and warm beer.
They sit on the rocks and peer into the water,
and they can't see their death masks
reflected in its surface,
but I can.

At night,
they build illegal fires to keep warm,
and the river is like tar,
opaque with secrets.

They have never seen the water hungry,
its yawp gaping wide and terrible.

Their mistake is not in calling the river beautiful,
      but in assuming its beauty
            is benign.

## **Threnody**

And when we put him in the ground for good,
like farmers planting unfamiliar crops,
I thought death was one of many stops:
a different suit of clothes, a change of mood.

A life is not consumed like firewood,
reduced to ash by flame that wails and pops;
a scrap must still remain, or so I thought.
I smelled the fresh-turned earth from where I stood.


But now, the worms have long been at his box
and he has not been anything but gone,
and maybe that is why a casket locks,
to keep the living always moving on.

We plant our flowers, on their fragile stalks,
so something is alive on graveyard lawns.

## **Breakfast of Lunatics**

On a morning in March,
I am hungover and twenty-one
in a temporary apartment that offers
the illusion of a home.


I have two rats and a mouse,
an honor role GPA,
and a dead boyfriend.
I offer the illusion
of being a person.


      The phone is ringing,
          but
   I can't seem to stomach
the possibility of another person's voice,
       and
  I can't seem to stop worrying
  the people who care about me.


I am curled like a dried leaf
on a cheap mattress,
holding hands with a ghost.
I am only passively alive,
and it is a form of surrender
    I cannot afford
        for much longer.

Other people say
this can make me bitter
or it can make me better.
They say everything
happens for a reason.

      Other people say
      a lot of stupid shit.

It is a morning in March,
and I am a salted field.

> I am not worth
> my own skin,
> but I am alive
> anyway.

So I take an aspirin
for the headache.

I answer the phone.

## **Alternate Ending**

Last night,
I dreamed you were in a coma
for all the years
you've been dead.

Your family called to tell me
they were taking you off life support.
       He's not getting better,
            they said.

It never gets better,
I told them.

I woke up
wondering which was worse:
the way it happened in my dream,
or the way it happened for real.

## Blue Notes

Rat knows how to play the flute.
He learned after the Pied Piper
used the same instrument
to lure so many of his brethren
to their demise.

He plays their elegy
outside the Piper's window.


        The Piper's name is Ern,
and he has papered the interior of his home
        with sheet music.

When he sleeps, the tails of rats
choke the melody from his throat.
He has begun to see them
during waking hours.


      Rat plays on;
his stone-smooth fingers moving
like depressed typewriter keys,
stringing together the letters
of the lost names he mourns.

    Ern sharpens his blade
against the softness of his own gut.

## Beyond the Cut Mark

When someone has been dead
      for a long time,
the shape of their absence
becomes ill-defined.


You cannot know
what their life would have been
in the time that's intervened
since their death.

There is no telling
what you might be missing,
and so you imagine
that it is everything.


The edges of the void
bleed outward.

 It will catch you
in the jaws of its lack;

     if you let it.

## **Beauty Marks**

I shave with cheap, pink razors:
      six for a dollar.

I prop my legs
across the bathtub's parted lips,
like the awkward angles
of utilitarian bridges
yawning over rivers.


The choreography of my hands
      is automatic,
as though I am playing my own body
      like a violin.

The blades sound rough
against my dry skin,
like someone scraping frost
from a winter windshield.


I am never as kind
to my body
as I should be.

I kid myself
that things like this
keep me tough.

The cheap razors
dot my legs with blood,
but I wear these wounds uncovered,
      like badges,
         like dares.

## **Tracey: An Elegy**

This morning,
he told me
you had died.

Your life had been
relapse and remission
for seven years,
so it shouldn't have been a surprise,
but somehow it still felt sudden.

Your being gone
was still a shock.


Time eroded our friendship
as unceremoniously as it does
so many others,
        but this morning
        I thought of you:
dyeing your hair red
in your boyfriend's dorm room,
and listening to Scarlet's Walk
in our basement apartment,
and wearing my pirate shirt.

I can't stop believing
I might still find you
        at these intersecting points
            of time and space.

## Relearning the Body After Rape

Pull the blanket down
and let your feet find the floorboards
                    again.


Bathe yourself
with hands that are not weapons.


        Burn your sheets
        if you must.


Wipe the condensation from the mirror
and resist the urge
to search your face
for some justification
of the wounded shriek
that cannot find its way to your mouth.


When your flesh feels as foreign
as so much portioned meat
upon the butcher's scale,
do not indulge the desire
to cleave it from your bones.

        It still belongs
           to you.


Understand you will never
look as scarred as you feel.
This is a kind of passing:
        a sort of blessing,
           a sort of curse.

Bring the geometry of your body
        out of shadow.
The space you take up
is the best evidence
of your claim on your own life.

Do not stop holding
others accountable
for the difference between invitation
and trespass.


Unmarry the cause and effect
between touch and recoil,
        not because you must,
        but because it is a freedom
        you deserve.

There are chapters of survival
that will never feel safe,
   but your body
is not a sarcophagus;
it is a suit of armor.

On some days,
the bravest thing you do
   may be
to believe this.

## Radiotoxin

You can call me
Chernobyl.
It's close enough to the truth.

    I am fluent
    in the language
    of warning.

Scorched shadows
litter my landscape,
and the charcoaled branches
of my orchards
will bear no fruit.

    My only season
    is nuclear winter.

    My only crime
    is being a victim.

No number of iodine tablets
will save you
from my fallout.

## **Grasshopper Mouse**

I see predators
        everywhere
smell the stink of someone else's blood
          on their muzzles
feel the shred of their claws on my back


        survival as privilege
        applies only to prey

        survival is intrinsic
        to predators


the supposed-to-be
    of prey
is submissive
is flight over fight
  is lay down
    and die


it would be dangerous
for you to assume
I live according to
supposed-to-be

it would be dangerous
for you to assume
I have failed
    to evolve

## Lamb's Blood

I'm told
it is no longer
appropriate
to let the steel show through
your strength.

Instead,
it is admirable to be soft
in your resilience,
like stalks of wheat
rooted against the wind,
like the locked muscles
of pastel-clad ballerinas
on their toes.


World ...
you should have thought of that
    before
you exploited
all that's soft in me
for the sake of nothing
I will ever understand.

You have grizzled my gentle
between the gnash of your teeth.
None of it was strong enough
to survive you.

I will not be ashamed
of the scar tissue I earned
by staying alive.
I dress it in rhinestones
and call it chain mail.
Your teeth tattooed
the word "tenacity"
across my back,
and I wear it like a warning.

*Philosopher Kings*

I will not apologize for the times
I had to choose between kindness
    and survival,
for refusing to keep turning my cheeks
until they are slapped off my face.


I sacrificed all my softness
at the altar of your appetite.
It pooled in your mouth
    like blood.

It is a relief
to have it gone.

## A Spell for Victor Frankenstein

The first thing you will need
is to be a certain kind of lonely,
the kind that finds no solace
in companionship
and disdains the ease
with which people trip across
the face of the world.


You must see well in the dark,
it is where your work is:

> the gathering of parts,
> the stitching of skin
> onto different skin.

You must learn to live
like the worms and the rooks.


Understand that your ambition
is not a child of anything pure.

It hungers for all that is left
of your humanity,
and you cannot pay it
with the fever of your labor.

Instead, it will beat its price
from those you have sacrificed
to the distraction your work demands.

If you are in love,
understand they are forfeit.

If you have friends,
you will find their still bodies
within steel caskets.

*Philosopher Kings*

When you've decided it's worth it,
let your audacity bear fruit;
let it rise from the slab,
        all crooked limbs
        and mottled skin.

When you meet its mismatched eyes
        with your own,
                ignore the whisper
                vibrating your skull
                like a trapped bee,
                asking which of you
                is more human.

## **Allegiance**

our bodies
are the bricks
in the wall
the mortar
is our blood
our piss
our vomit
there is no roof
there is no hearth
it is a monument
to defeat


in time
we will become
a field trip curiosity
a new generation
will look upon
our decayed ruins
and feel
a detached sense of horror
or disgust
or (please not) admiration


there are no windows
the doors are locked
and the walls are too high
to be scaled
this is the house
    we built
may we be judged
accordingly

## Alpha Centauri

Triads
have a long history
of significance.
Humans like the artifice
of our lives
to be easily divisible by three.
We like trinities
and trilogies,
the comfort of three things
functioning as one,
like the way you look
like a single star
when viewed from the vantage point
of a still field on a distant planet.

Astronomers call you
A, B, and C,
but I call you
maiden, matron, crone,
and I wonder if you are
born of the same contained flame.
I wonder if you watch us
the way we watch you,
on blankets in backyards,
through telescopes
in multimillion-dollar laboratories.

Can you tell us
if we matter
as much as we think we do?

Our light is too dim
to reach across all the time
it would take for us to get to you,
but maybe our ruin will be bright enough
to pierce the distance.

Maybe our supernova will leave a scar.

## **Armadillo Heart**

A psychiatrist once told me
that I think in worst-case scenarios;
my mind
is always a fist
and never just a hand.

Something in me
cannot unclench itself,
will not allow me
to feel safe in this world
because I have not been safe
in this world.

When the phone rings,
I hear death.
When men smile at me,
I see malice between their teeth.

I have been caught unaware
before.
I looked away
and suddenly the world
had a knife to my throat.

I refuse to be surprised
by my own devastation
        again.

## Documents of Barbarism
**To write poetry after Auschwitz is barbaric.** -*Theodor Adorno*

You critics who object to poetry about the Holocaust
on account of its beauty,
you say beauty makes sense of things,
and we can never presume
to make sense of genocide.

I wonder if you have never seen
New England's autumnal leaves,
the sun-sky-hued funeral gowns of the trees.
People make pilgrimages to watch them fall,
and what sense is there in a thing
that is most beautiful in death?

Who of us understands the full-fringed eyelashes
        of a stillborn child,
or the music played on doomed instruments
      while the deck of the Titanic
        split like a ripe plum?

Into what logical language
can you translate the determination
set into a young teacher's jawline
as she becomes a human bullet shield
in a classroom
of a Connecticut elementary school?

If you object to the beauty of Holocaust poetry,
let it not be on the grounds of logic.

Do you think Paul Celan made any sense
of Margarete's golden hair,
of Shulamith's ashen hair?

Wir trinken und trinken,
and still we are thirsty.

For most of us,
the Holocaust will always be remote,
a chasmic maw
of unfathomable depths.

We cannot look at it directly,
but we can try to imagine
the variable keys
groping the tumblers of locks
that secured snow-filled houses.

We can be reminded of what it means
      to survive our own history.

## Sums and Parts

The mirror fogs,
but I don't wipe it
          clean.

Instead, I open the bathroom door
and wait for the temperatures to level.

Eventually,
my reflection emerges
like a ghost in a smoky bar.


What I notice
about my own body is never
what other people see
          first.
The shaft of metal in my eyebrow
has long been absorbed
into the ordinary landscape
of my face,
and the cluster of scars
on my stomach
from an old body art project
seem no less mundane
than cellulite or stretch marks.

Sometimes, I forget the color
of my own eyes.


Instead,
I notice how my right eyebrow
is slightly off-center.
I finger the crescent moon scar
on my calf,
taking pleasure in its pale sleekness–
so much more delicate
than the rest of my skin.

I do not so much comb my hair
as unleash its intractability.

In the dissipating shower steam,
I paint the lids of my eyes
like an Egyptian burial mask.


The body
makes for poor math,
and the addition of all these features
yields only a nonsense sum.

I am cohesive only because my parts
happen to hang upon the same body.

    You can look at me
as though I were an equation ...
    but I have never had
        a solution.

## Imaginary Numbers

My mind resists math,
not because it's difficult,
but because I have so rarely
been able to apply its formulas
to my experience of being alive.


So many of math's foundations
depend upon deriving
answers that are singular and absolute.
    Three
    minus
    three
    equals
    zero
  every time.

But what if, one day,
    three
    minus
    three
    equals
    nineteen?
        or negative six?
        or cellar door?

The equation of my romantic relationships
between the ages of eighteen and twenty-one was
    abuse
    plus
    abuse
    plus
    death.
The first integer was never static,
and glowed red like the digital display
    on a bomb,
  5, 4, 3,
  0,0,0.

*Philosopher Kings*

The second integer was
a negative number.

Every time I added myself to him
less of me was left.

The third integer was one hundred and eighty,
which is the number of seconds
it takes for someone to drown.

Of course, the human body
is an unaccountable variable,
so it's possible he was
one hundred and sixty-seven,
or one hundred and ninety-two,
and you can see how the math
becomes complicated,
becomes impossible.

These numbers added up to nothing,
which is to say their sum
could have been anything,
and might as well be nothing
if what you're looking for
is an answer.

Math insinuates itself
into my daily life.

It tips my waitstaff,
and converts my students' grades
into percentages,
and calculates the number of syllables
in this poem,
but I have never been able
to fit myself within its formulas.

Too much of what I am
is irreducible into
usable data.

## Flight Plan

The airport is pumped full
of TSA-approved air molecules,
filtered at regular intervals.
Recorded messages remind me,
each hour,
to guard my bags
against bombs or cocaine.
The default setting here is suspicion,
and I should feel safe,
but I don't.


Yesterday, a plane crashed in San Francisco.
The news footage flashed
severed tail,
charred nose,
broken landing wheel
abandoned on the runway.
The plane simply hit the ground
too hard upon landing.


I am always most unglued
by the moments in which the plane lifts,
      retracts landing gear,
      and surges upward
at an angle to the benign tarmac,
becoming a canister of human beings
      ascending in defiance
      of our wingless bodies.

## Hometown

At the Jimmy Stewart Museum
in Indiana, Pennsylvania
a six-foot stuffed rabbit
flanks the door:
a Buckingham Palace guard
for the hopelessly sentimental.


Inside, there is a movie theater
lined with straight-backed chairs.
I hope for Vertigo,
but it's The Spirit of St. Louis.
I abandon my seat
to walk the labyrinth of exhibits,
the chronology of someone else's
    'Wonderful Life'.

Entire rooms are replicated:
here, an office,
here, a parlour.
One display boasts a bed
he slept on.
His military uniforms hang,
preserved,
like carefully collected chrysalides.

I am far from home.
My own life spins its wheels
fruitlessly in New Hampshire,
while I contemplate a plastic trophy
with worn engraving
and wonder if we are defined
by the things we hold onto.
I am lonely here
like lost socks are lonely.
I return to the theater
and close my eyes
to the small comfort of a familiar voice.

## Emblems of Grief
*For Richard Girard*

The fire trucks pass,
their sirens silent.
This dumbstruck quietude
is the dirge of your procession.


The first time I saw you bury one of your own,
I was still young enough
to feel awkward at funerals.
You caught my eye and winked.
In uniform with your feet planted wide,
you looked indelible.
It's the only moment of comfort
I remember from that day.


You brought me daisies
when my boyfriend died.
Silk ones,
you said,
so I would always have them.
You must have known
I'd need something that would last.


Now, I am hundreds of miles from the place
where they will pray over your body,
where bagpipes will mask the sounds of mourning.
I am too far away to hear the silent sirens,
but I have sent you daisies.
They aren't silk;
they will not last,
but they are the bearers of my gratitude and grief.
They are not enough,
but their fragile stalks
are all I can offer.

## Today's Brass Tacks

The day has been
unyielding,
and the painted metal bars
of the park bench outside the library
are bruising their signatures
across my thighs and spine
while I thumb the newsprint pages
of the latest anthology
for the latest class
in which I am enrolled.

I'm distracted by a squirrel,
gnawing at half an orange
pinioned anomalously between tiny paws.

I pull from the box of crackers,
     passing for lunch,
  and cast a few at my feet,
and it's the greatest pleasure of my day.

My life has been distilled
down to such simple tasks:
     read,
     write,
     listen.

I am grateful
   now
for things like
     telephones,
     and sleep,
     and squirrels,
  gathered like believers
at the foot of my meager offering.

## Pocket Watch

Emily Webb is yearning
    for her lost life

        on
          stage

while Mother Gibbs implores,
      Be silent.
        Lie still.


The theater seats
are thinly-padded,
straight-backed,
and ill-suited
for long productions on August afternoons.


Grover's Corners
is the closest I have been in months,
and it's not the New Hampshire I know,
but it's one I'll accept.


Far from home,
I have been restless
and malcontent.
I have strained against the fit of my life
like a bad suit.

The stage manager palms his pocket watch,
and I am reminded of how
few things are immutable.

So much of this will not come back
again.
      Be silent.
      Lie still.

## In Context

My professor says
Darth Vader
is a philosopher king.

I feel at home here
for the first time in eleven days.

## Lawn Ornaments

Today,
there was a wild rabbit on the quad,
brown camouflage betrayed
by the white trim of an upturned tail.


There are rabbits everywhere
in western Pennsylvania.
I have been here for two months,
and am no less amazed
by their casual cameos
in the bushes bordering the dorms.

I wonder if this is how tourists feel
about seeing moose
in the north woods of New England:
those antlered, shaggy beasts
that appear suddenly on isolated roads.

      There are no moose
      in western Pennsylvania.

I conjure one to mind:
the majesty of a muscled trunk
on slender legs,
the sloping bridge from ears to nose.

      I am homesick
      for so many things.

## Scrapper

I carry half my body weight
       in books.

One of them digs into my kidney
through the canvas wall of my backpack.
       Even at the university,
         I am a beast of burden.


Some days feel like dark magic:
I am articulate in the classroom
and formidable on the page.
The Phaedrus reads like Stephen King.
Most days are more dust and less luster.

Sometimes, my words spill tangled,
exposing my disarrayed thoughts.

Classroom floundering
is a sort of nakedness.
I am a gyrating fish:
out of water and
stripping my scales against
the confines of a net.


By Thursday,
I am parched at the lip
of the weekend's oasis,
but on Monday morning,
my muscles are taut like guitar strings
out of tune.

My books are at my back
like sword and shield.

I am battle ready.

## Fever Dreams

Today, three people collapsed
against the Pittsburgh heat,
according to the news.
The night is charged with it,
and I lie restlessly on a dorm room mattress
while the silence beats like blood
behind my eyes.


Outside, my fitfulness radiates away,
and I walk the quiet streets
absently clasping a cluster of blue flowers
torn from the branch of a nearby bush.
Everything is strange:
the city, the heat, myself.
I am not tethered to the world
in any of the usual ways.


Later, my skin is damp against the artificial chill
of the dive bar off Philadelphia Street.
Drinks are served in cheap plastic cups;
a dart game unfolds at the far end of the room;
my blue flowers are limp against the tabletop.

When the overhead lights
fall into yellow pools
    at last call,
the outlines of my body
fall into sharper relief,
and I am once again reassured:

       I take up space,
       I have not evaporated
         into the heat ...

   of this uncomfortable night.

## Friday Service at the Caffeine Cathedral

The barista's moustache
is waxed into sculpture,
a pair of ram's horns
capped with teacup-handle loops.
The counter is an off-center island,
rooted amidst mismatched tables,
hemmed in by local art.


They have chalked a sign for us,
a hand clutching a microphone.
It stands on the sidewalk
    like a road sign,
a symbol meant to convey
 a gathering of people
spitting spells into the rising darkness.


We help stack the chairs
when we're done
before spilling onto the street
still vital and untapped.

The barista wipes the chalk from the sign,
but the ghosts of the lines remain
    like hazy signatures.

## Small-Town Murder Cowboy

Every summer,
it's the same guy
sitting in the doorless entry
of a shabby storefront
that masquerades as a tanning salon.

He looks like Buffalo Bill
from Silence of the Lambs,
with a limp, nineties shag
and ill-fitting denim shorts
cut too high above the knee.

He holds court
in a dirty, beige patio chair
while a dark hallway
unrolls behind him
and I wonder,

    in passing,

who would be willing
to follow a guy like that
out of the daylight?

## The Patron Saints of Coffee Cups

The early morning men
at the fair-trade coffee shop
are not who you'd peg as the target demographic.
They wear cracked boots and weathered faces.
Outlines of wallets
and lighters
and packs of cheap cigarettes
are faded into the pockets of their jeans,
like bleached tattoos.


They trade stories
and share raucous laughter
while they banter with the baristas
behind the counter.
Their scarred hands,
folded around the bells of beige cups,
look like disarmed weapons,
look like prayer.


They lift their mugs to the morning,
baptizing their bristled beards in coffee.

## Our Lady of Libations

The windows rise in rows
above the dive on the ground floor,
relics of a time when this used to be
      a low-rent hotel.

I can imagine the windows lit
like a hundred mismatched candles,
the vitality of hard-knock lives.

Tonight, they are all dark,
the promise of their intrigue
long since snuffed out.
The whole building
could be mistaken for condemned,
except for the erratic, neon sign
that burns brightly against the grey,
and draws us like moths.

It is a place choked by the ghosts
of so many things that didn't last,
      and to last
is the grail we quest for every day.

When we have spent our ambition,
      we return here,
   to the gut of an old hotel,
to the only part of the building
      where the lights
show no sign of burning out.

## The Garden at Dawn

I am back from the bar
as Thursday passes its torch,
and the quad is populated
with wild rabbits,
tails turned up
so the undersides glow like milk,
ears still, like radio antennae
tuned to a frequency I can only guess at.

The intermittent light of fireflies
peppers the dissipating darkness,
and I had almost forgotten
fireflies were real.

And what purposes have wild rabbits
        fireflies
but glossy eyes and gentle illumination?

And what purpose has a night like this
but to dash out a question mark
at the edge of our reality?

## **Praying at the Altar of Fruition**

There is a certain strain
of magic
when the research for the night
is nearly done,
when I am making a couch
of the library armchair
with my bare feet cast
over one of its arms.

Like everyone else,
I burn to be brilliant.
Like everyone else,
I fear I am mediocre.
These Romulus and Remus thoughts
are the backdrop of my labor:
each one trying to win the day,
fighting dirty for the right
to be the better brother.

Some women
want to bear children,
to watch their skin grow taut
around another nervous system.
Instead of that,
I swallow lines of text like seeds.
There is a nascent forest
       in my brain,
scratching against the shell of my skull.

As the night wrings itself out,
I put down my pen.

      Like everyone else,
        I hope:
   the work has been thorough,
the notes make sense in the morning,
       that any of it
         matters.

## One More Rough Beast

I didn't mean
to flay both my knees
on the morning of my first set of doctoral exams.


My roommates were alarmed
when I returned from a morning run
trailing blood and sweat,
but there was nothing for it.
The exams began at nine,
so I cleaned up
and we went.


It was cold for May,
the day heavy with pewter-bellied clouds,
       but I wore a skirt
        so I wouldn't bleed
  through the knees of my pants.


When we got to the classroom,
the program director eyed me with amusement.
"This is what grad school does to you," he said.

I sat at a computer
and propped one mangled leg
on the chair next to me.
I took my exam papers
and started typing.

## Fool's Mate

When Bobby Fischer won
*'The Game of the Century'* at thirteen,
I wonder if he could see death play out
        in front
                of him,
so many decades into the future.

Chess demands a kind of logic
        so intricate
it can appear as clairvoyance.


We fight age like a disease
because it reminds us of dying.
To be alive is to play chess
with invisible pieces,
never knowing when you're in check,
but always assuming you must be.


Bobby Fischer
refused treatment for renal failure
at the end of his life.

    Maybe he knew
there were no moves
        left.

## **Elegy for Dead Architecture**

the stale air
in the summer stairwells


the classroom chairs
in which I sat
for aching hours


the clatter of wooden doors
shrunken too small
to quite fit their jambs


the urgency of ordinary ambition
in the voices spilling out
into the otherwise quiet hallways


      it is,
      all of it,
      gone now


Leonard Hall has fallen down,
one more London Bridge


I didn't expect there to still be rubble,
      but there was,
a landfill of bricks and steel and glass,
contained by a chain-linked perimeter:
ersatz walls for a phantom building


in places, the mortar still held,
larger pieces of exterior walls
resisting their own disintegration

at the rear corner
of this *'once-was'* building,
a lone doorway still stood,
intact and hemmed by a border of foundation,
in refusal of its own irrelevance


behind the library, the new humanities building
turns its grey face to the sun,
its banks of windows
      like the hundred eyes
      of a wonderful monster


    the lobby is vast
    the ceilings are high
    the elevators are quiet


        it is everything
        we always said
        we deserved


and yet,
    I am drawn to the rubble,
    for reasons
    I cannot name


and yet,
    I am compelled
    to reach for the handles
    of the orphaned doors,
    to cross the threshold
    of this building's death rattle.

## To Call the Muse

Let your insomnia
perspire abstract art
onto your sheets.
Resist the nervous impulse
to peel face from skull,
but when the embedded itch
becomes unbearable, rise
in damp and nervous glory
to pace the soothing chill
of the floorboards.


Quell the moan
of your own need
with infomercials and silver static.
Match it scream for scream,
cancel it out.
When the cold cavern
in front of your spine
devolves into a morass
of rage and accusation,
attempt to fill it
with stale cereal and flat beer.


Understand you will always feel
like you're playing dress up,
but that doesn't make you
a liar.

Accept that no one will call your name
until you speak it yourself,
until the reverberation
is so far reaching
both ancestors and descendants
stop to listen.

*Philosopher Kings*

When you have exhausted
your own resistance,
when you have forgotten
to be embarrassed,
when there is nothing else left
to distract you from the fever
of a thousand hornets in your brain...
you will let her come

        And then,
        you will begin.

## The Girl Who Spoke Albatross

When the ill-fated mariner
hunted the prey of his own demise,
she translated
the bird's final majesty.
She gathered feathers from the deck of the ship,
and wove him a headdress
so the fates could find their mark
with ease.


She never told him
what the albatross said.


When the crew shriveled with thirst,
the dead bird's young descended
to carry the girl away.


From the sky,
she saw the ship of the dead approach.
She called no warning to the lone figure below.

## Nor'easter

It has been snowing for eight hours,
and the colored Christmas lights
reflect against the whitewashed windows
instead of casting their glow out into the storm.

Beneath the clouds is an artificial darkness,
a sort of half-light that exists
outside the trappings
of the collectively accepted reality.

Outside, the snow absorbs sound
like the vacuum of space.

When I heave the trash into the dumpster,
I find a raccoon making his supper
out of table scraps.

We share a moment of incredulity
at the strange silence of the false twilight.

## **Fighting Words**

The first time we met
      in battle,
ambition cut the nascent ideas
from the womb of my mind
and threw them, squalling,
    upon your dais
like so much embarrassed nonsense.
I was too uncertain
to let my wounds weep freely.

The next time,
I was ready.
I fought harder
for the full gestation
of my thoughts.
I had better weapons
and bluer bruises.
I wasn't afraid
to spill my gore
when I knew
it would be worth the mess.

The last time we meet
      in battle,
I will be an obelisk
of pale and gleaming scar tissue
marring your vista with my elegance.
I will be a honed hammer.
I will have
no softness left
to exploit.


    The last time we meet in battle,
you won't even notice you're bleeding
      until I'm already gone.

## Lazarus Season

A New England autumn
is a sort of phoenix suicide.
The season slits its own throat
and lets the blood litter the ground
        like regalia
to herald the false death
        of winter.

After months of bleakness,
the thaw is not so much rebirth
        as resurrection:
an ostentatious display of triumph,
        a vernal smirk—

Did you think you could keep me
        gone?

## Tires for Tombstones
**on a painting at the Artists' Hand Gallery**

These woods are where
trucks go to die.

A graveyard of rusted chassis' in place of monuments,
collected wheels adorned with clots of mud.
There's a sacredness to the juxtaposition
of industrial steel and rampant weeds,
to the hulking, metal machines
driven through the trees and left to their slow rot.

The roots grow through their open spaces.
It's almost like they belong here.

## Coppers

At the end of the season,
the pickers come
to strip the fruit from the branches.
They balance on the highest ladder rungs
with three apples in each hand
at a half-cent per piece.


All autumn,
the orchard rows
are full of well-fed families
who pay for the quaint privilege
of gathering their own food.
They will not translate
the number of apples they pick
into pennies.


Just before the leaves fall,
the pickers arrive
to exsanguinate the orchard
and pick their teeth
with the pittance they are paid.

By the time their apples
appear in your grocery store,
they're already gone:
        another state,
        another crop,
        another penny harvest.

# Flux

and suddenly
it is September
and I am in a new office
at a new school
and I cannot recall
when summer ended


I drive an hour to work
through the kind of woods
I grew up in
and sometimes
there are ambiguous quadrupeds
in the road at night:
foxes
fishers
anemic coyotes


sometimes
I scarcely recognize my life
in the aftermath of upheaval
that seemed to take no time at all

there was no time
to put away the yesterday


something died
and was reborn
on the seam of August and September
and I cannot say
what it was

## Cartography

I am standing in the middle
of a stone walkway
on a college campus
for what may be the last time,
and imagining all the threads of myself
caught in the teeth
of the places that have been my homes.
I am thinking what a wonder
it is I have not yet unraveled
into nothing.


These threads are the lines
between cities and states

When I picture my blood vessels
beneath my skin,
I think of maps
superimposed over other maps.
When I close my eyes,
I exist in so many different places
at once.


I am a deconstructed artifact,
and my far-flung parts
comprise the only evidence
I have ever been alive.
I close my eyes and
I am learning to dance barefoot
on the toes of my father's wingtips,
and watching a cloud of bats
rise out from beneath a Texas bridge,
and then I'm falling asleep
in the air-conditioned chill
of a Pennsylvania library,
and learning how to be born
on a stage in a bar.

*Philosopher Kings*

I am standing in a walkway
on a college campus,
and the grit of the bricks is catching
on my loose threads,
and I am falling
     to pieces
       again,
and this is how I become
   more complete.

## Amorphous Relics

My blank spaces
are what I've been taught
to be ashamed of.

They are what's least
of value
to anyone else:
        unsculpted expanses
        of colorless clay,
          the places where I am
          unmade.

The sculpture of my humanity
has been the work of my life
   and I no longer know
how to lay down my tools.

And yet, there are places
I will not touch,
final reminders of something intrinsic
       and unconstructed
    that used to be everything
         about me.

## Elegy for Boots

purchased for two dollars
at a secondhand store,
a half size too large
worn into classrooms and basement bars
baptized in equal parts
by summer sweat and winter slush
treads packed with beach sand
and graveyard grass,
with gravel from the train tracks
held firm in pits at three
Nine Inch Nails shows
left footprints on sidewalks
in Texas, Wisconsin,
New Hampshire, Pennsylvania
patched with marker and electrical tape
laid to rest in the belly
of a metal donations box,
empty, but well-traveled

## Acknowledgments

The author gratefully acknowledges the previous publication of the following poems:

"In Context" Red Flag Poetry
"Blue Notes" Contraposition
"Drugstore Banquet" Carcinogenic Poetry
"Tires for Tombstones" Carcinogenic Poetry
"Oscillating Frequencies" Threepenny Review
"Break, Definition Of," The Belmont Story Review
"Our Lady of Libations," The Belmont Story Review
"Welcome to Civilization" The Belmont Story Review
"Praying at the Altar of Fruition" The Oddville Press
"Elegy for Dead Architecture," Scarlet Leaf Review
"Cartography," Scarlet Leaf Review
"Feast" Scarlet Leaf Review
"Tracey: An Elegy" Bloodroot Literary Magazine
"Beauty Marks" DASH
"Lamb's Blood," The Charles Carter
"Flight Plan," The Charles Carter
"Relearning the Body After Rape" The Charles Carter
"Green Monday" Anti-Heroin Chic
"The Poet at Eighteen" ZiN Daily
"Flux" The Wild Word
"Fever Dreams" The Wild Word

## Author Biography

Cara Losier Chanoine is a college English professor and the author of *How a Bullet Behaves* and *Bowetry: Found Poems from David Bowie Lyrics* (Scars Publications 2013 and 2016). Her creative work has appeared in *The Threepenny Review*, *Red Fez*, *WINK*, and other publications. She holds an MFA in Creative Writing and a PhD in Literature and Criticism. Her scholarly work particularly focuses on the relationships between text and performance in live poetry, an interest partly fostered by her experiences as a four-time competitor at the National Poetry Slam. Her article "Ethnopoetic Transcription and Multimodal Archives: Toward a More Comprehensive Approach to Slam Poetry Scholarship" appears in the Winter 2023 issue of *Oral Tradition*.

www.carachanoine.wordpress.com

www.ingramcontent.com/pod-product-compliance
Lightning Source LLC
Chambersburg PA
CBHW072105110526
44590CB00018B/3320